A VIEW FROM ABOVE

IRELAND

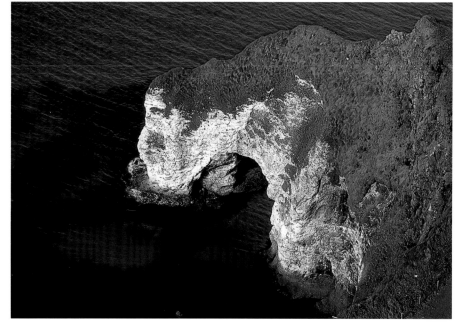

vmb
PUBLISHERS

A VIEW FROM ABOVE IRELAND

TEXT
Christopher Moriarty

PHOTOGRAPHS
Antonio Attini

EDITORIAL PROJECT
Valeria Manferto De Fabianis

GRAPHIC DESIGN
Patrizia Balocco Lovisetti

1 Green, the emblematic color of Ireland, is well set off by the white chalk cliffs of Carrick-a-Rede in Co. Antrim.

2-3 The ruins of Dunluce Castle on a cliff-top on the Antrim coast have defied waves and wind since the 17th century.

4-5 Ashford Castle, now a luxury hotel, was built for a Guinness lord in the 19th century.

6-7 Lough Neagh, the largest lake in Ireland, encompasses an area of 150 square miles (388 sq. km).

8 Small fields and bare rock characterize the landscape of the three Aran Islands off the coast of Co. Galway.

9 The 19th century saw the building of a great many lighthouses on the coasts of Ireland. This one is on the Co. Donegal cliff top.

10-11 The steep-sloped island of Cobh in Co. Cork overlooks a safe deep-water anchorage for vessels crossing the Atlantic.

12-13 Standing at the head of a lonely bay in the estuary of the River Moy, Co. Mayo, Rosserk Friary was built for Third Order Franciscan friars in the 15th century.

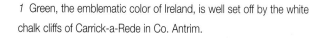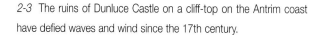
vmb
PUBLISHERS

VMB Publishers® is a registered trademark property of Edizioni White Star s.r.l.

© 2008, 2010 Edizioni White Star s.r.l.
Via Candido Sassone, 24 - 13100 Vercelli, Italy
www.whitestar.it

ISBN 978-88-540-0825-0

1 2 3 4 5 6 14 13 12 11 10

Printed in China

C O N T E N T S

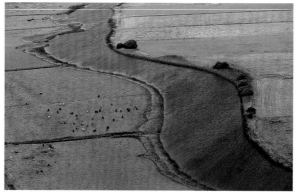

The memory of flying over Ireland is of green fields, brown hills, silver rivers, blue lakes and blue sea – above all a land of contrasts, always changing, never dull for a moment. Perhaps something of this landscape has entered into the soul of the people. While there may be ruggedness in places, the country and climate are essentially welcoming and, most of all, romantic and mystical. At its root is spaciousness – seemingly endless space with a feeling of timelessness. But that is only half the picture. Irish people began to leave their mark on the landscape five thousand years ago, before the pyramids of Egypt were built. Our flight over the fertile lands of the east makes a special obeisance to Newgrange, the hilltop temple built, overlooking the sacred River Boyne on the request of some of the first cattle barons. Across the green water meadows from the temple is the beautiful visitor center, built in the 1990s, where specimens of the best in Stone Age culture and modern art and design sit comfortably together.

We might go across the midlands towards the west to enjoy a view of Lough Derravaragh. Lying between steep green hills, it was the dwelling place for three hundred years of the Children of Lir, turned by the enchantment of a wicked step-mother into four swans, who sang songs and told the people stories of ancient times.

Equally we could head to the southeast and *Dublin's fair city, where the girls are so pretty and I first set my eyes on sweet Molly Malone*. Molly Malone is long dead, but the girls are as pretty as ever and Dublin has grown from a Viking seaport, to a citadel of Anglo-Norman invaders, to a gracious city of 18th-century masterpieces of Classical architecture and finally to a vibrant metropolis that changes and spreads year by year.

Renewal is everywhere, most of all in the Docklands. Ships have grown bigger – you may spot the biggest car ferry in the world at anchor, waiting to take passengers across the Irish Sea to Wales. In the 18th century, sailing ships berthed far up the river, a little way downstream of the house in which that great Dubliner James Joyce set his poignantly romantic story *The Dead*. The docks moved downstream from the city center as the ships got bigger. The latest move left great spaces available for development and gleaming new office blocks and apartments share the riverside with inviting tree-lined walkways and enticing pubs and restaurants. But don't forget that the old resides comfortably with the new everywhere in Ireland, and Dublin retains a most delightful old-world flavor.

As we go farther south, the suburbs thin out and increasingly large green spaces separate the growing villages and townships from one another. There is greater space to left and right. To the left is the Irish Sea, its shores liberally supplied with inviting beaches, thronged with people

on warm summer days. To the right the great chain of the Wicklow Mountains begins and so does space on a grand scale. County Wicklow calls itself The Garden of Ireland and this is no idle boast. One of its most famous inhabitants was St Kevin, who established a monastery in Glendalough, the most romantic of all the valleys of Wicklow. Our flight can zoom in over the splendid round tower, which has dominated the valley for a thousand years.

Halfway along the Wicklow Mountains, we might take a right turn and cross a succession of river valleys. First comes the Slaney, renowned in history for its part in the republican rising of 1798. Then we see the Barrow which has an especially interesting pattern from above, thanks to the building of weirs, locks and canals to take horse-drawn barges from Waterford Harbor, on the south coast, to inland towns.

Beyond the Barrow lie the Slieve Bloom Mountains, a range of deep, romantic, forested valleys with beautiful rivers and waterfalls. And in folklore the Slieve Blooms are renowned as the childhood home of Finn McCool, poet, warrior and magician, whose origins go back more than five thousand years to the times of the hunter-gatherers.

As you go south of the Slieve Blooms, you will see in the distance the Devil's Bit, a flat-topped mountain with a great chunk missing from its summit. The scientific explanation of its existence is not much less wonderful than the traditional tale that His Satanic Majesty snapped it up with his jaws. Geologists date its excavation to the Ice Age, when all of Ireland, except its highest mountains was covered with a field of ice, flowing slowly from the north. As the ice melted, torrential streams flowed over the land and created gorges and deep valleys, of which the Bit is one of the most spectacular.

But the older story tells that the Devil spat the Bit out again and it landed in the plains nearby to form the Rock of Cashel, Cashel of the Kings. No chieftain could resist building a stronghold on such a hill, whose precipitous sides discourage attack and whose height commands a marvelous view of the surrounding green and fertile land. It became a great center, first as the palace of the kings of the province of Munster. In the course of time, they handed it over to the Church and the great Gothic cathedral was built. It flourished as a place of worship until, it is said, the archbishop grew tired of riding his horse up the hill and had the roof removed. In spite of the desecration, Cashel remains one of Ireland's greatest shrines to the memory of fifteen hundred years of Christian worship.

Before we leave the fertile and populous lands of the east and south, with their busy towns, we must look down over the city of Cork, built

on the steep sides of the River Lee. Flying over Cork is a helpful way of getting to know it, because the river divides into two very similar streams – extremely confusing to a first-time visitor on foot. Above the southern branch towers the 19th century cathedral dedicated to St Finbarr and on the northern branch stands the Church of St Anne with its immortal *bells of Shandon that sound so grand on the pleasant waters of the River Lee*.

Westwards from Cork, spectacular parallel ranges of hills spread out beneath us. Created by the crumpling of the earth's surface in a north-south direction, their wild and barren tops contrast with green and fertile valleys and they finally plunge into the Atlantic Ocean to the southwest. Rivers and ice scoured out deep valleys between them and then the sea level rose, making a series of deep inlets and cutting off their tips to form rugged islands. The Blasket Islands were the home of a community of fishermen and farmers and a remarkable collection of writers and storytellers. Two rocks, that rise from the ocean like cathedrals, are the Skelligs. On the summit of the larger of the two there still stand the beehive-shaped stone huts that monks built a thousand years ago. The smaller one is white and lively, the summer home of more than ten thousand gannets.

Following the coast to the north brings us to the Shannon Estuary, a magnificent sea inlet, bordered by evocative small towns and harbors and leading to the city of Limerick, with its Anglo-Norman cathedral and castle, built to guard a ford over the Shannon, the biggest and most exciting of all the rivers of Ireland. At Limerick we have a difficult choice. We might follow the river to the north to see its many beautiful lakes and busy waterway, big enough to accommodate all the thousands of people who fish, surf, sail or make a leisurely journey through Ireland in houseboats.

The alternative is to fly past Shannon Airport and out to the Atlantic coast, perhaps dipping down to watch the dolphins which live in the estuary and perform to human audiences. This is County Clare, one of the richest in natural wonders and folk tradition. The little fishing village of Doolin is the greatest center for gatherings of traditional musicians. The great Cliffs of Moher rise like a stone wall from the boiling surf below. Then comes the Burren, a vast area of gray limestone rock, enlivened all over by green patches of pasture and hazel wood and brightened in spring and summer by wild flowers growing in the rock crevices.

A flight over the three Aran Islands is one of the highlights of a trip around Ireland. They were brought to international fame in the classic film *Man of Aran* by Robert Flaherty, whose people lived there, by the playwright J. M. Synge and by the islander Liam O'Flaherty. Here the old, Irish-speaking world embraces the new: each of the three islands has an airstrip. Do not fail to land on one of them, nor must you miss the colossal Iron Age fort of Dun Aengus perched high above the ocean on the edge of the biggest island of the three. The Burren is bordered to the north by

Galway Bay, with the city of Galway at its head and the far-famed Galway Racecourse where, it is said, most of the major political decisions of the nation are taken between races in the refreshment tents.

North of Galway Bay is the marvelous wasteland of Connemara, a great seaside region of bog, studded with lakes and interrupted by magnificent mountains. Flying around them or over their peaks is an experience never to be forgotten. County Mayo, equally packed with mountains, bog and lakes, lies to the north of Connemara. In its lowlands is Knock International Airport, the brainchild of the local priest and custodian of the shrine, built to celebrate a vision of the Virgin Mary which appeared on the wall of the old village church. The white cone of Croagh Patrick, Ireland's most holy mountain, stands above the sea on the north Mayo coast and, out beyond it, are the Ceidhe Fields, Stone Age field boundaries discovered when the peat, that had overwhelmed them, was cut away in the 20th century.

County Sligo has yet more mountains, above all the snake-like ridge of Ben Bulben, chosen by the poet W. B. Yeats for his burial place and a literary shrine ever since. We fly through the Barnesmore Gap in County Donegal, so narrow that you feel you could lean out of the window and touch the cliffs as you pass. The county has more than a fair share of lakes and mountains and includes the beautiful valley which forms Glenveagh National Park. Then we cross the border into Northern Ireland and perhaps the most famous piece of seacoast in the entire island. It centers on the Giant's Causeway, a promontory composed of man-size blocks of basalt, with a backdrop of stupendous cliffs. South of the causeway is the River Bann, where the remains of Mesolithic people, the earliest inhabitants of Ireland have been found and, in very much more recent times, the home of the poet Seamus Heaney. The Bann flows from Lough Neagh, the isle's greatest lake and, south of Lough Neagh is Belfast city, a great industrial center in contrast to the cities of the south. The flight gives a great view of the shipyards of Belfast, birthplace of many of the 20th-century's greatest vessels. Most of them enjoyed long and distinguished lives – but the most famous of all was the *Titanic*.

We finish our circuit of Ireland by going low over the Carlingford Mountains, where the champion Cúchulain single-handedly defended the province of Ulster against the armies of Connaught, under the command of the redoubtable warrior-queen Maeve. Then south over the Hill of Tara, famed in history and legend: historically the seat of the high kings of Ireland, in legend the scene of many a battle with the forces of the underworld and, somewhere between legend and fact, the place where St Patrick converted the pagan high king to Christianity.

The picturesque thatched cottages of the past have been replaced by comfortable bungalows and the villages that were decaying as recently as fifty years ago are full of life and growing again. A new sense of prosperity has spread through the old country. But the space remains and the old traditions, the ancient castles and churches and the uncrowded landscape are cherished with greater love and care than ever before.

IRELAND

FORTY SHADES OF GREEN AND SILVER

One tradition describes the four provinces of Ireland as 'four green fields' and a song recounts our 'forty shades of green.' That color dominates the landscape and features, too, as the emblematic color of the nation. The great expanses of brown peat bog are interrupted by patches of green, as are the gray limestone wastes of the Burren and the purple-headed mountains. It has a lot to do with the Irish weather. While the sun may shine for long periods, there is no seasonal period of drought. The weather is as changeable as the landscape that it has painted.

For thousands of years oak forest covered the greater part of Ireland, with ash, pine and hazel providing variety in places. Farming communities slowly replaced the forest with green pasture, a process which accelerated suddenly in the 17th century, leaving the country almost bare of woodland. Pockets survived around the lakes of Killarney, in Glendalough and other remote places. Today they are lovingly cared for, with much of their areas enclosed in national parks. Killarney, even without its oak and yew woods, would be a very special place and rightly deserves its position as the longest-serving and best known tourist center of all. One great, island-studded lake, bordered by a great house and parkland and a romantic ruined abbey, lies cradled by magnificent mountains, rising to Ireland's tallest peak which just tops 3280 feet (1000 meters).

In Ireland you are never far from the sea and never far from mountains.

Even the lowlands are broken everywhere by hills, large or small. Although the mountains are relatively low by world standards, they share one essential feature: they are either too high or too wet or too steep for people to live on their slopes. So nobody has ever succeeded in building houses or roads over great expanses, nor has anyone bothered to divide up the land there and a wonderful wilderness remains to welcome people in search of solitude.

Some of the smaller hills have very special effects on the landscape and the view from above reveals this in a way that is not possible from the ground. The most remarkable of all are the drumlins that form a winding ribbon from coast to coast in the north midlands, ending in the west in Clew Bay. There they have been invaded by the sea to form a pattern of green islands. The drumlins are egg-shaped hills, aligned by the passing of great glaciers in the ice age. They effectively block the passage of rivers, resulting in a myriad of small and large lakes, especially Lough Erne, whose waters, like those of Clew Bay, are liberally scattered with islands.

The River Shannon was created by the punishment of the fair maiden Sionna, carried away on a sudden flood when she had the temerity to bathe in a sacred pool on the flanks of the Cuilcagh Mountains. The flood carried her all the way to the sea at Limerick, and the waters spread over much of the land in its track, forming three great lakes, Allen, Ree and Derg and countless smaller ones. Loughs Derg and Allen reflect the mountains that surround them; Ree lies in more open country. Apart from a short, skittish section in the mountains and a final plunge to the sea, the Shannon flows placidly between its lakes and has provided a passageway into the midlands from time immemorial. Its importance shows clearly from the air in the form of the ruins of ancient monasteries, large and small, on the islands and by the riverside. Nineteenth-century canal construction joined the Shannon to the Erne and today the two great rivers and their lakes provide a fantastic waterway, with more than enough space for the thousands of canoes, yachts, fishing boats and cabin craft that make it one of Ireland's loveliest spots for quiet recreation.

The Shannon and its tributaries fail to drain a great area of the midlands. The shallower lakes of times long past were transformed to swamps, to fens and finally to peat bog. The latter half of the 20th century has seen the exploitation of the peat, forming an amazing landscape of flat brown, inhabited only by colossal yellow machines which crawl over its surface, scraping away layer upon layer of peat for use as fuel. Happily for the preservation of this rare landform, the machines can't cut to the bottom and, when they have done their work, the displaced birds and wild flowers return – except in the special cases where the lakes of old appear once more or where grassland and forest grow again.

The 18th century saw three great changes to the landscape, all three having a special appearance from the air. The most lasting one was the enclosure of open spaces, turning them into a patchwork of large or small fields divided up by hedges or by stone walls in cases where the soil was too thin to allow trees and shrubs to thrive. Most of the hedges are of hawthorn which makes beautiful white ribbons in early summer when its flowers bloom. The planting of forests began again, together with the building of high walls around many of the demesnes of the rich. And two great industrial highways were built across the country – but they were waterways, not roads. The Grand Canal and the Royal Canal both travel across the midlands, joining the River Liffey to the Shannon, allowing cargo and passenger vessels to travel from coast to coast. Superseded by the railways of the 19th century and the roads and motorways of the 20th, they have joined the Shannon and Erne as havens of tranquility.

Peace is the essence of Ireland – and it shows from the air in the wide open spaces that separate the busy towns and villages. Even Dublin, the biggest and busiest city is small enough to allow its citizens easy access to the wilderness. The fertile lands are populated by contented herds of cattle and sheep. To an increasing extent, forest is clothing the less productive areas and purple heather or white bog cotton add color to the highlands. All combine to offer a rich feast to the eyes of those who see Ireland from above.

21 The Shannon, Ireland's greatest river, flows placidly through water meadows. Rising in the mystical Shannon Pot on the Cuilcagh Mountains, the greater part of its 200 mile (320 km) course is through the lowlands where it has formed a highway for thousands of years.

24 and 25 The Gweebarra River, following a long narrow defile, meets the Atlantic Ocean on the lonely coast of Co. Donegal, the north-western corner of Ireland. It lays down its burden of silt, derived from ancient quartzite rocks, to form mile upon mile of silver strand.

26 left The drumlin landscape of Co. Down is part of the range of low green hills which extends in a wide band from coast to coast in the northern midlands of Ireland. Composed of gravel and clay, the hills were formed by the movement of a great ice field.

26 center The drumlins in places blocked the natural flow of the rivers and created lakes, large and small. Submerged in part, the small hills stand out above the water to form islands and promontories. Upper Lough Erne, in Co. Fermanagh, is a delightful maze of lake and islands.

26 right The islands of Lough Erne were densely covered with forest in prehistoric times. Farmers cleared the woodland over the millennia – with a sudden increase in clearance in the 17th century. Now 20th-century re-afforestation is changing the scene once more – but uses trees from the Pacific coast of North America.

27 Named by Viking invaders in the 9th century, Strangford Lough is a great inlet of the Irish Sea in Co. Down. The drumlin hills again give it a great character of islands and promontories. It is a fine wintering ground for geese, duck and wading birds which nest in the Arctic.

28-29 By the banks of the River Erne, these small fields divided by hedges are a characteristic of much of the landscape of Ireland, providing a charming patch-work pattern. In spite of its timeless appearance, the system is relatively new, developed by 18th-century landlords.

30-31 Lough Gill is one of the most beautiful of the many lakes in Co. Sligo. The poet W. B Yeats, whose ancestors lived in the county, celebrated its tranquillity in one of his most famous and best-loved poems The Lake Isle of Innisfree.

32 Church Island, Monks Island and Fairy Island in Lough Gill commemorate centuries of historical Christian worship – together with a
little folklore and memories of the 'good people' who make occasional forays from the pagan spirit world.

33 Church Island, like its companions on Lough Gill, is densely covered with native woodland: ash, hazel, oak and other species. Scarce
on the mainland, these trees are secure on the islands and give an
example of how the land looked in prehistoric times.

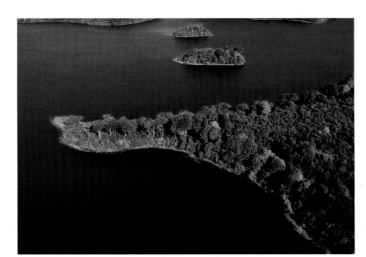

34 To the north of Sligo Bay the long limestone ridge of Ben Bul-

ben stands above the lowlands. The land to the south of the bay

is rich in the remains of temples and burials constructed by the

Neolithic farmers who dwelt there five thousand years ago.

36-37 In Co. Roscommon, the home of the redoubtable Queen Maeve and the starting point of *The Cattle Driving of Cooley*, one of ancient Ireland's greatest sagas, old jostles with new. The traditional farm house on the left has been supplanted by an affluent dwelling.

37 A golden crop of barley awaits harvesting in Co. Roscommon. Its destination may be as animal fodder or perhaps it will be roasted to give the dark colour of a glass of Guinness or fermented, distilled and matured for years as the basis of Irish whiskey.

38-39 A lonely shepherd makes his way across the green sheep pasture of Co. Roscommon. The mild and moist climate of Ireland ensure that grass grows at all times and both sheep and cattle can graze throughout the year.

40 The waters of Lough Carra in Co. Mayo are highly charged with lime which covers the rocks by the shore with a white crust. The surrounding land was for centuries the property of the family and ancestors of George Moore, who distinguished themselves in politics and literature.

41 The waters of Lough Carra are pure and clear but reflect a pale green color from the surface. Rich in the essential element calcium, they are the habitat of the finest brown trout in the country and a haven for sport-fishermen.

42-43 The karstic land of Co. Mayo produces wonderful patterns of grey rock, the dark blue of deep lakes and the greens and yellows of rare forms of vegetation. The expanses of bare limestone rock which constitute karst are found only in the counties on the Atlantic seaboard.

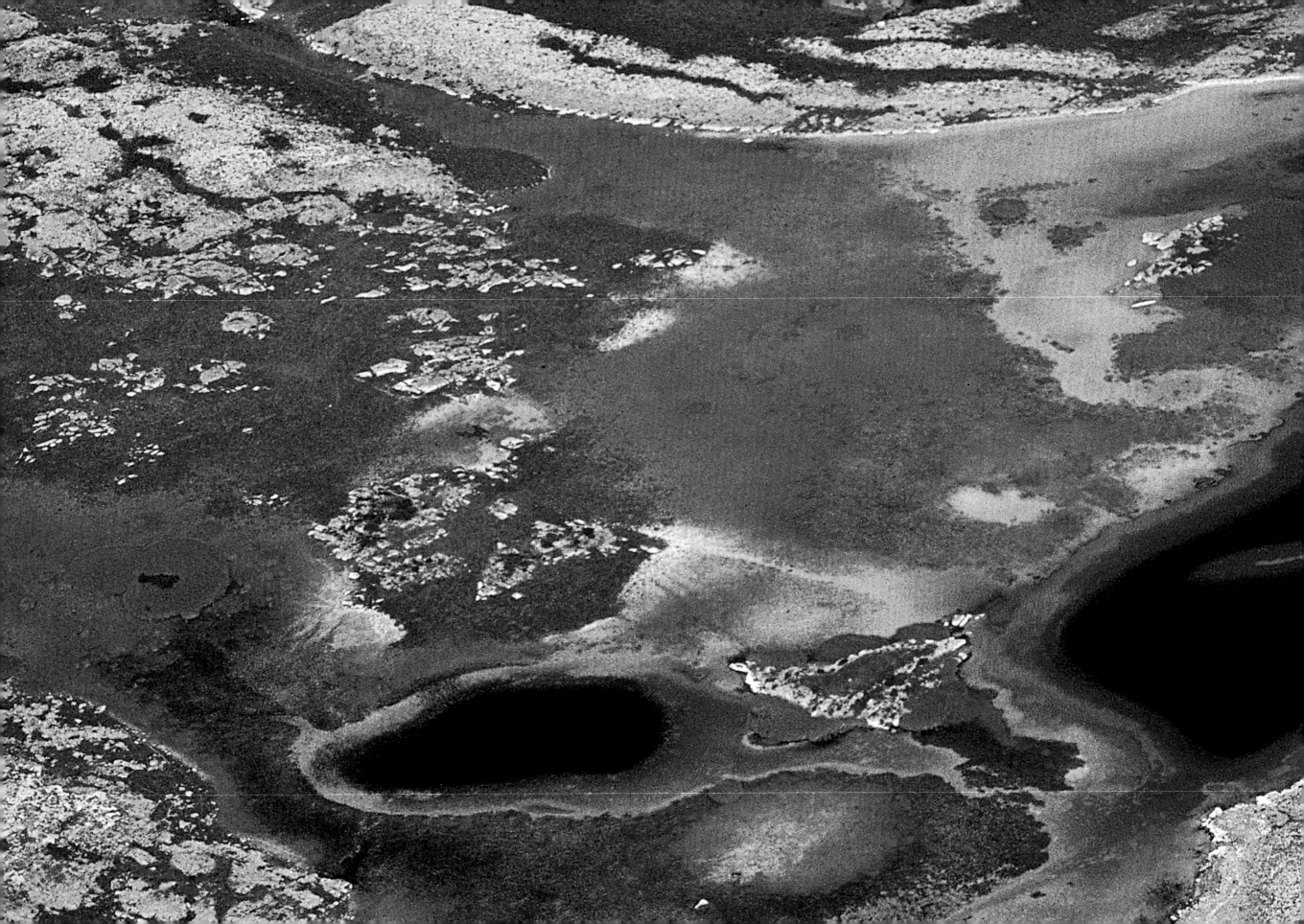

44 left A major part of Ireland's greatest waterway, the River Shannon, developed in the 20th century into one of the most popular venues for pleasure cruising. Families from all over Europe come to hire comfortable craft and enjoy the stillness of a world of water.

44 right Lough Corrib, extending over 65 square miles (168 sq. km) is the second biggest lake in Ireland and one of the most popular as a venue for superb fishing for trout and pike. Holiday cottages have taken over in many places from the old farm houses.

45 Field boundaries and farm-working make the pattern on the dry land of a promontory in Lough Corrib. Lime-encrusted stones, reed bed and swamps border the deep water. Winter brings thousands of wild duck of many species to the lake.

46 left and 47 Although nearly all the woodland of Ireland had been cut away by the end of the 17th century and has never been fully replaced, the countryside never seems to be devoid of trees. Ash and other species grow in the hedges that form the field boundaries.

46 right The tracks of a mowing machine follow the line of a hedge in the countryside near the town of Athlone in the center of Ireland. Not far away the poet Oliver Goldsmith was born and spent his youth. He made an immortal description of the land and its people in his poem The Deserted Village.

48 Once a busy time for the entire community when the hay was cut by hand and stacked by women and children, haymaking today is a solitary task for one man, his tractor and his baler which deposits great cylindrical bundles of winter fodder for his cattle.

49 Use of the combine harvester, during the second half of the 20th century, has led to the enlargement of fields by the removal of hedges and the creation of a more open landscape than prevailed for the preceding two hundred years. A more ordered and geometrical appearance has come about in these lands of Co. Westmeath.

50 Until the 20th century cattle were the basis of the Irish economy.
Rich green pastures with grass growing from January to December
ensured that beef of the highest quality could be produced to feed
both the people of Ireland and their neighbors in Great Britain.

51 While most of the land was cleared for cattle-rearing, patches of
woodland were retained by landowners, as a source of firewood and
as cover for birds such as the woodcock which provided sport and
food in winter. In the 18th and 19th centuries hardwoods, especially
beech and oak, were favoured.

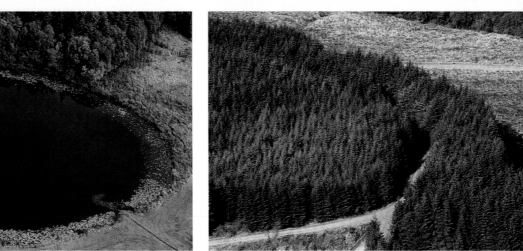

52 Both the small island and the woodland are man-made contributions to the landscape. The island is a crannog, constructed from stone placed in the shallow water to make a secure dwelling for a family and their cattle. The woodland is of sitka spruce, imported from North America and the most successful tree in Irish forestry plantations.

53 A lonely tower dominates the scenery in a clearing in the woodland on the Slieve Bloom Mountains. Thousands of years ago in the fastness of these hills the hero Finn McCool was reared in secret – to become one of the most famous of all Ireland's legendary figures.

54-55 The Burren of Co. Clare, an area of 140 square miles (360 sq. km) of bare limestone, is one of the most dramatic land-forms in Ireland. Enlivened by occasional small green fields and pockets of hazel wood, it abounds in wild flowers, many of them unknown in other parts of the country.

55 One of the many islands in the estuary of the River Fergus which connects to the Shannon. Cattle or sheep are brought over by boat to graze the summer pasture. In winter the estuaries of Shannon and Fergus provide a haunt for thousands of migrant birds.

56-57 Patterns of blue and many shades of green make a picture of a seaside farm in Co. Clare. The great estuary of the River Shannon, with its countless indentations, is a favorite spot for fishing and water sports.

58-59 The lowlands of Co. Cork (Ireland's largest county) are home to rich farms with large fields. Red-painted hay-storage barns add to the 'forty shades of green.'

60 The hedges that surround these fields and farms in Co. Cork – as in all other parts of the country – are vital refuges for wildlife. Many species of song birds such as blackbirds, chaffinches greenfinches and robins live there winter and summer, flying down to the fields to hunt for insects and worms and enjoying an added bonus of the berries in autumn. Hawthorn is the dominant species of shrub in most cases, supplemented by hazel, guelder rose and many others.

61 Ancient and modern ways co-exist in this Co. Cork farmstead. The green pastures bordered with hedges dotted with trees have been that way for more than a century. But the house is new and so are the tractor-produced cropping lines in the tilled fields.

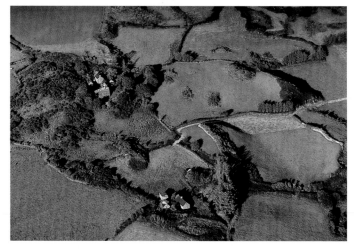  

IRELAND
TRACES OF TIMES PAST

The sacred River Boyne flows through County Meath, one of the most fertile regions of Ireland. A flight towards the east, down the river within the county gives an unforgettable view of some of the most renowned and striking ancient monuments of Ireland – and is something of a microcosm of five thousand years of its history.

But, for the sake of a chronological approach, we might begin our trip in the neighboring County Westmeath and the nearby catchment of the River Shannon with its mysterious, Y-shaped Lough Derravaragh. Between the arms of the Y the great archeologist Frank Mitchell discovered traces of an encampment of Mesolithic hunter-gatherers, the first human inhabitants of Ireland who had reached our shores eight thousand years ago. They were the first industrialists, making flint arrowheads for trade as well as for their own use, but they left no conspicuous traces of their civilization – so we will just have to imagine them, catching eels and trout with their flint-tipped fishing spears.

Fifteen miles to the northeast, the view appears of a range of green hills, dotted with sheep and, much more importantly, with thirty cairns of gray stones. These are passage graves, built to contain the mortal remains of the Stone Age folk of Neolithic time who introduced a vitally different way of life to Ireland, three thousand years before the time of Christ. They cleared away patches of the forest that had previously covered the whole of Ireland, herded cattle, raised crops and left monuments to their dead in every part of the land.

Not far from these, the Loughcrew Hills, a tall steeple announces the town of Kells. The steeple dates back to the 18th century – but it has for near neighbors a tall round tower and an ancient church with a steep, pointed stone roof. And, among the tombstones in the churchyard, no fewer than three Celtic crosses. Tower, crosses and church are each more than a thousand years old and represent a peak of achievement of the Celtic Church, which had been established in Ireland since the 5th century, when St Patrick came to preach to the scattered communities of Christians that lived here.

Kells is on the River Blackwater and, when you follow it downstream to where it joins the Boyne, you may divert a little and fly over the Hill of Tara where legend, history, romance and archeological fact all combine to make one of the most famous Irish sites. Nobody lives on this great, green hilltop and perhaps no one ever did. But people have celebrated it as a sacred gathering place for five thousand years. A little green hump is a passage grave – a Neolithic building which is proof of this great antiquity. A pair of interlocking circular earthworks are the remains of a great Iron Age palace constructed about two thousand years ago. Tara was the throne of the High King of Ireland for a thousand years or more. Legend tells that St Patrick converted the king there and Christianity rapidly took over the whole country.

If you follow the Boyne upstream for a little way, you will see by the riverside the mighty fortress of Trim, a great square tower protected by river, cliffs and massive walls. It tells the story of the invasion of Ireland by Anglo-Normans and the beginnings of British rule which would be accepted by some and endured by many from 1167 until 1922. Downstream from Tara, the Boyne takes a sharp bend to the south and, within that bend, are three great mounds of earth. The central one is Newgrange, famous throughout the entire world. Not only was it built by a Neolithic community five thousand years ago, it is decorated with sophisticated, abstract sculpture and, above all, contains a central chamber approached by a tunnel through which the sun shines for a few minutes as it rises on the winter solstice.

Across the river, you can see the fields where the Battle of the Boyne was fought in 1691 – a rather small battle on Irish soil but, remarkably, a decisive one between the royal houses of France and the Netherlands. To the north is a sanctuary of more peaceful memory: in a secluded valley you may trace the outline of Mellifont Abbey, the first house of the Cistercian monks in Ireland. They introduced Gothic architecture and something of a revolution in agriculture – besides the significantly reforming religion.

Finally we head for the port of Drogheda, passing a magnificent new suspension bridge and an equally splendid 19th century railway viaduct. Between them is the medieval town and beyond it the Boyne makes its majestic way to the sea.

The Boyne Valley presents a microcosm of all the major phases of Ireland's long history. But traces of the past stand out in every part of the country. Away to the west are the Ceidhe Fields with traces of the field boundaries of the farmers who lived there five thousand years ago. All over the country tall stone tower houses stand in dignified isolation. They were built in the 14th and 15th centuries, when settler cattle barons felt insecure.

Some of the castles, like Bunratty, are very much alive and well and host medieval-style banquets. Monasteries were suppressed by order of the English King Henry VIII in the 16th century – which meant that most of them were abandoned sooner or later by their communities. But they were well-built and traces of their churches and cloisters stand out everywhere. Narrow round towers with pointed roofs indicate the Celtic foundations which flourished until the 12th century. Gothic towers show the influence of the continental orders that came to replace them.

After centuries of strife, Ireland became peaceful in the 18th century and landowners made themselves large and comfortable Classical-style houses rather than castles. Hard times fell on many of them – but the Celtic Tiger has come to the rescue and the past few years have been a fantastic time of restoration both of the great houses and of the magnificent gardens that their owners created.

63 Three castles, joined by a curtain wall, were built on Three Castles Head in the 15th century. Forces of wind and wave rather than enemy attack has reduced the number of surviving ruins to just one.

66 The ruins of Downhill Castle on the coast of Co. Derry (or Londonderry). Built by the wealthy and eccentric Frederick Augustus Hervey, Earl of Bristol and Bishop of Derry in 1780 and enlarged by successive owners, it was reduced to ruins in the 1950s.

67 The cliff-top Mussenden Temple, part of the 18th century demesne of the Earl Bishop of Derry has been restored. It was built as a library and also had a lower room which the Earl Bishop, in spite of his Episcopalian position, allowed his Catholic tenants to say Mass.

IRELAND

68 Built on a precipitous headland on the north coast of Co. Antrim, Dunluce Castle served both as a secure refuge from land-based attackers and as a look-out post over the sea to the Scottish islands which are clearly visible in fine weather.

69 A dramatic view of Dunluce Castle, showing (to the left) the open ends of the walls where the cliff collapsed and fell into the sea, bringing part of the castle with it. Tall gabled roofs with chimneys and mullioned windows show the architecture of the extending of the old castle which took place in the 17th century.

70 Romantically situated on the very shore of the Irish Sea in Co. Down, Quintin Castle was founded in medieval times. It was rebuilt in the 17th century, fell into decay and was finally enlarged on a magnificent scale in the 19th century.

71 The original medieval castle that stood beside Quintin Bay is completely hidden by the elaborate battlemented towers and curtain walls that were built in the 19th century. Its function then was simply to impress the neighbours by its opulence, rather than to defend anything.

72-73 Devenish in Lough Erne is one of many lake islands on which monks of the early Celtic church established monasteries. The lakes at the time were highways through the land. Over the centuries several religious orders settled on Devenish and substantial traces of their monasteries remain.

74 Built by the British statesman Lord Palmerston, the Victorian-Gothic castle of Classie-Bawn became the holiday home of Earl Mountbatten of Burma, the last Viceroy of India. He was assassinated in 1979 by Irish Republican extremists, while on a fishing trip nearby.

75 Parke's Castle, beautifully situated on the shore of Lough Gill, Co. Sligo, was built on the site of an earlier tower house owned by the Gaelic chieftain Brian O'Rourke. After centuries of disuse, it has recently been restored by the Irish government and opened to visitors.

76 and 77 Ashford Castle was built in the 19th century around an ancient castle in an exquisite setting by the banks of Lough Corrib in Co. Mayo, one of Ireland's biggest and most beautiful lakes. Now a luxurious hotel, it offers golf, fishing for superb trout and even training in falconry.

78-79 Moyne Friary is one of two built close to the River Moy in Co. Mayo. Begun in 1460, its ruins are more extensive than those of its neighbor Rosserk. The friaries flourished until the 16th century when their use was forbidden by the England's King Henry VIII.

80 Farmleigh House on the edge of Dublin's Phoenix Park owes its present form to extensions to an earlier house carried out in the 1880s to the order of the Earl of Iveagh, an hereditary proprietor of the great Guinness brewery. Purchased by the Irish government it now serves as a venue for meetings of dignitaries.

80-81 Luttrellstown Castle in Co. Dublin was a medieval fortress, but began to be enlarged and converted into a luxurious dwelling in the 18th century. The 19th century saw its reaching its present size and appearance. It is now a country-club-style hotel and golf resort.

82 The Stone-Age temple of Newgrange is the most distinguished of all the pre-historic monuments of Ireland. Built five thousand years ago it pre-dates the pyramids of Egypt. The white façade is made of quartz stones found buried when the building was excavated for repair work in the 1970s.

83 Newgrange is technically known as a passage grave: within the mound a long passage, made from huge stones, leads into a domed chamber in which cremated bone was found. A special opening above the entrance allows the sun to shine into the chamber when it rises on the winter solstice.

84 left and 84-85 Dun Conor on Inishmaan, the middle of the three Aran Islands, is a splendid stone fort which contains the foundations of a number of huts. The construction is of 'dry stones' without mortar and has withstood two thousand years of Atlantic gales.

84 right When people first traveled to the Aran Islands off the coast of Co. Galway, the land was densely strewn with large stones, deposited by glaciers in the Ice Age. They used the stones to make field boundaries and to construct colossal fortifications.

86 The stone castle on a hilltop on Inisheer, the smallest of the three Aran Islands, and the ruined houses nearby are associated with defences against an invasion by Napoleon Bonaparte – which never took place.

87 The Napoleonic defences on Inisheer are set in a rectangular enclosure. An ancient irregularly-shaped wall surrounds the 15th century stone castle which was built by an unknown warlord. The Aran Islands are a sanctuary for the Irish language and many traditional ways of fishing and farming.

88 The buildings on the Rock of Cashel, which rises steeply from the fertile plains of Co. Tipperary, were constructed over a period of more than a thousand years. The round tower with the pointed roof was built in the 10th century. Cormac's Chapel, with its twin square towers was dedicated in 1134 and is the finest Romanesque church in Ireland. The central cathedral dates to the 13th century. Cashel was a royal palace in prehistoric times, presented later to the Church.

89 The riverside priory at Kells, Co. Kilkenny was founded in 1193 by the Anglo-Norman warlord Geoffrey fitz Robert de Monte Marisco for the Augustinian order. The 13th century towers and walls place it among the most extensive monastic ruins in Ireland.

IRELAND

90 The home until the 1980s of the Earls of Dunraven, the building of Adare Manor began in 1831 and continued for a period of thirty years or more. It stands beside the River Maigue amidst exquisite gardens and parkland in Co. Limerick.

91 Adare Manor is a country-club style hotel in Co. Limerick, set in a great estate with parkland and gardens. It offers its guests golf, health and leisure activities.

A VIEW FROM ABOVE

92-93 The parkland of Adare Manor, conceived in the 18th century as an open space with shady trees for the comfort of horses and cattle, makes a perfect setting for the championship golf course that has taken over from the livestock of past times. The Franciscan friary of Adare (which is now surrounded by a golf course), was dedicated in 1464 to the Archangel Michael.

94 One of the stone forts that are among the greatest ancient monuments of Co. Kerry. Built entirely of dry stone, the massive walls are 12 feet (3 m) or more in thickness and as much as 18 feet (5 m) high. Most of these forts are dated to the Iron Age.

95 Leacanabuaile, near the mouth of Dingle Bay in Co. Kerry, is a relatively small stone fort which excavations showed to have been in use about a thousand years ago.

97 Lismore Castle, the Irish seat of the Dukes of Devonshire was built by order of the 6th Duke in the 19th century to the design of Joseph Paxton. One of the most splendid of all the Victorian castles, it stands on a cliff-top overlooking the River Blackwater.

IRELAND
CITIES OF GRACE AND CULTURE

The city of Armagh has a particular charm of its own, with its two cathedrals exchanging theological arguments from their secure positions on two neighboring hilltops. They look good from the ground – but the view from above adds a very special dimension. We can see a third hill not far away with a grass-covered mound rather than a stone cathedral. It is Emain Macha, one of the most important centers of Celtic rule and of pagan worship in the Iron Age. So Armagh effectively links Christian worship with the Celtic religious practices that it replaced. The city developed around the older cathedral in the 18th century and the Episcopalian Church of Ireland built its archbishop the magnificent Classical palace that stands near the cathedral, surrounded by trees and green lawns. In recent times the archbishops moved to a less august dwelling and the palace is now the property of the people rather than of the Church. On yet another hill, another fine Classical building is the astronomical observatory. Armagh is unique amongst the cities of Ireland in other ways: besides its abundance of hills, it has neither sea nor a great river. It is also the ecclesiastical capital and, having enjoyed that distinction for fifteen hundred years, refuses to recognize the political border put in place in 1922.

Fifty miles to the northwest is the city whose name depends on your political or religions persuasion. If you are Catholic and nationalist you call it by its old name, Derry. But if you are a Protestant and supporter of the union with Britain, it is Londonderry. Whatever name you choose, the city, in common with Armagh, has a pagan origin. The name means 'oak grove' and the oak was sacred to the Druids. The great St Columba annexed the oak grove – peacefully by all accounts. He was a very forceful preacher with a reputation for taking up arms with great success in defense of his principles. London came into the name in the 17th century when a consortium of London merchants was given the old town as a gift. Their work makes the city every bit as unusual as Armagh. They surrounded their property with a defensive wall – making it something of a fortress – and built a new cathedral in Saint Columba's sanctuary. Having survived a siege (which was all too horrible but has taken a major place in folk history), the city has expanded and has long since gone far beyond its walls, crossing the great river estuary called Lough Foyle and spreading upstream and downstream.

Derry or Londonderry lies at the head of a beautiful sea inlet with hills on either side. So does the city of Belfast – but there the resemblance ends. The 17th-century walls of Derry are its most striking feature. A colossal yellow gantry is the first object to catch the eye in Belfast, the center of the great shipyards which developed in the 1850s. Unlike any other town in Ireland, Belfast is a child of the Industrial Revolution, based primarily on the manufacture of linen, but equally famous for ship and aircraft manufacture. Thirty years of sectarian strife came to an end in the 1990s. The opening of the superb Waterfront Hall concert venue in 1997 is a symbol of Belfast's reversion to its role as a city of culture and fun. The tight rows of small workers' dwellings contrast with the spaciousness of parks, university grounds and botanical gardens. There the great palm-house was a pioneering product of 19th-century engineering and the genius of the Dublin ironmaster Richard Turner.

Away to the west, the city of Galway is spreading over an increasing area of land, centered on a cluster of islands in the River Corrib, where it meets the sea in Galway Bay. Galway stands on the boundary between rich and poor, between wilderness and prosperity, separated by Lough Corrib, one of Ireland's largest lakes. The view from the air is of contrast between green pasture to the east and brown bog and mountains to the west. Older than Belfast but, as Irish cities go, a rather late foundation, Galway was established in the 13th century and ruled by nine 'tribes,' descendants of Anglo-Norman settlers but owing no allegiance to their former overlords. The 16th century saw a great development of Galway, based on its harbor and trade with Spain. The second half of the 20th century saw a transformation from easy-going provincial town to a capital of the computer industry. Despite these changes, Galway has not lost its old-world charm and enthusiasm for comfortable life at a gentle pace.

Little bits of old Galway survive, and the view from above gives glimpses of narrow streets, tucked away between the 19th-century shops and houses that predominate. The city of Kilkenny, on the other hand, still retains a great feeling of its medieval past. Its most ancient traditions go back to the 6th century and St Canice, who established a monastery there – to be replaced later by the rather squat Gothic cathedral that stands today. The Anglo-Norman invaders built a castle on a cliff top, to command a crossing place on the River Nore, which winds its way through the town. Rebuilt and greatly enlarged over the centuries and now an art center and museum with a beautiful green park, the castle looks down on the most delightful city that developed around it to become, in the 20th century, synonymous with all that is best in Irish craft-work and design.

The River Nore is one of three 'sister rivers,' celebrated in poetry in Elizabethan times by Edmund Spenser, and joining together to meet the sea in the great inlet called Waterford Harbor. In a narrow part, sheltered by steep hills, the Vikings established a seaport. Their name for the place translates as 'the ford of the god Odin' – but the settlers were converted to Christianity and built a cathedral. They also built a tower to guard the harbor, a tall round building on the quayside and it still dominates the scene, a more than thousand years after its foundation.

A VIEW FROM ABOVE

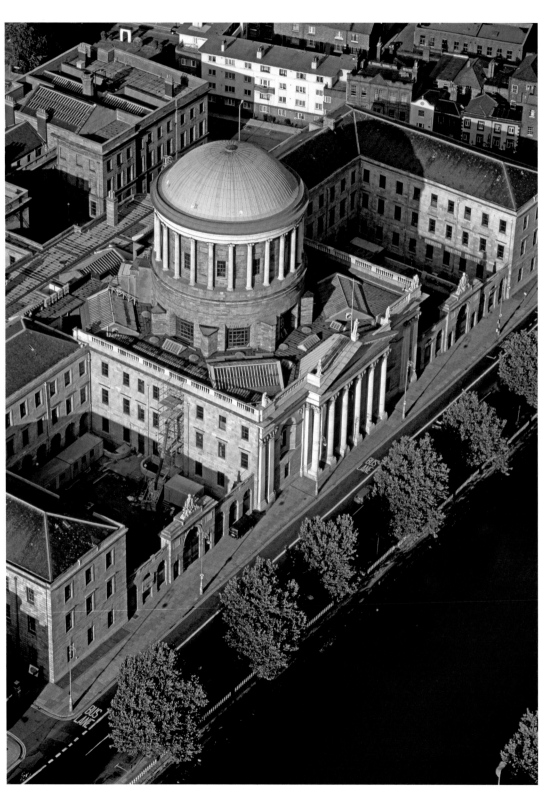

99 The medieval center of the city of Dublin was built on a high ridge overlooking the River Liffey and with a view to the south of the Dublin Mountains. The splendid 19th-century church is one of the dominant features of the skyline of the city.

102 The central law courts of Ireland are situated in the magnificent riverside building known as the Four Courts. Designed by James Gandon in the 18th century, the complex was severely damaged in the Civil War in 1922, and was restored and partially rebuilt in the 1930s.

103 The River Liffey runs from west to east to meet the sea in Dublin Bay. The 18th-century court house, with its copper dome, is one of the finest of Dublin city's public buildings. The majority of the old riverside houses have been replaced by 20th-century office blocks.

104 The Royal Hospital, Kilmainham on the outskirts of the city of Dublin was built between 1680 and 1687 as a home for old and disabled soldiers. Its public rooms were beautifully decorated and the whole building has been carefully restored. It now houses the Irish Museum of Modern Art.

105 Dublin University was founded by Queen Elizabeth I of England in 1592. The front square of its Trinity College contains superb buildings of the 17th, 18th, 19th and 20th centuries, including the magnificent Library which houses the world famous 8th-century manuscript Book of Kells.

106 The harbor of Dun Laoghaire was built in 1817 as a 'harbor of refuge' from the storms of Dublin Bay. It developed as a major ferry port, for travel across the Irish Sea to the Welsh port of Holyhead. In recent years marinas have been added to accommodate increasing numbers of yachts.

107 Overlooked by a medieval castle, Bullock Harbor is one of several built in Dublin Bay for sailing boats crossing between Britain and Ireland. Much too small for modern commercial vessels, it now serves as a popular yachting and fishing harbor.

109 The River Foyle flows below the city of Derry into the great bay
of Lough Foyle, an important British naval base until near the end of
the 20th century. The quays have been transformed to riverside walks
in recent years.

110 Stormont Castle was built in parkland on the edge of Belfast in the 1920s as the seat of government. The older City Hall is the municipal headquarters.

111 Belfast's elaborate City Hall dominates Donegall Square in the center of the town. Built between 1902 and 1906 to the design of Sir Brumwell Thomas its opulence is a symbol of the wealth of the city at the time, based largely on ship-building and the weaving of fine linen cloth.

112 The Queen's University, Belfast was founded in 1845, one of three provincial university colleges in Ireland conceived as multi-denominational establishments. Beginning with 90 students, Queen's now caters for 24,000.

113 The city of Belfast developed as a great industrial center in the 19th century. It was the home of one of the world's most renowned ship-building companies and the birthplace of the *Titanic*.

114 Armagh is a modern city which has developed from pagan beginnings in the Iron Age. The ecclesiastical capital of Ireland since medieval times, it is now the seat of Roman Catholic and Episcopalian Archbishops and has a cathedral for each denomination on two adjacent hilltops.

115 The Catholic cathedral of Armagh, dedicated to St. Patrick, is a magnificent Gothic revival hilltop building approached by a great flight of steps. Its building was begun in 1840 but not finished until 1873. The interior decoration is largely the work of Italian artists.

116 Sligo town stands at the head of Sligo Bay. It was developed by Viking seafarers and remained an important seaport until ships became too large for its shallow waters. The Catholic cathedral was completed in 1875.

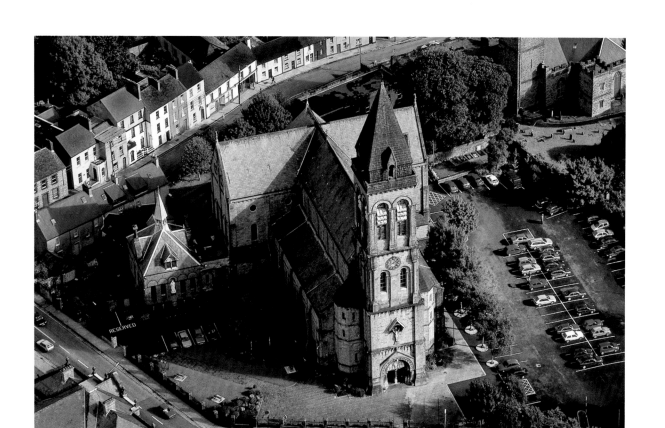

117 The River Garavogue runs from Lough Gill to the sea in Sligo, dividing the town in two. Sligo is an important cultural center, with museums and art galleries and strong associations with the poet W.B. Yeats and his painter brother Jack.

118 Athlone, in the center of Ireland, developed as a strategic town controlling first a ford and later a bridge across the mighty River Shannon. The castle first built in 1210 remained in use as a military barracks for more than seven hundred years.

119 Upstream of the Castle, the riverside in Athlone is dominated by the Catholic church, built in the 1930s. It stands beside a large military barracks. Beyond the fine railway bridge is the extensive Lough Ree. Athlone is renowned as a center for boating and fishing.

IRELAND

120 The city of Galway combines a romantic past as a trading post with medieval Spain with today being the capital of the computer industry in Ireland. Galway stands between fertile pastures to the east and barren moorland to the west and is something of a gateway to the great wilderness of Connemara.

121 Galway City grew up on a number of islands, formed where the short River Corrib divided into smaller streams. A multiplicity of bridges and canals are a special feature. Delightful traces of its 16th- century prosperity remain among the modern shops and office blocks.

123 Centered on the great castle founded in 1391 (and occupied by the same family until the 20th century), Kilkenny has all the charm of a medieval city. The castle, rebuilt in the 19th century, now serves as a museum, art gallery and concert hall.

124 Abounding in colleges and places of worship, the city of Kilkenny has played a major role in the development of Irish culture. Jonathan Swift, the satirist and author of *Gulliver's Travels*, was educated in Kilkenny College.

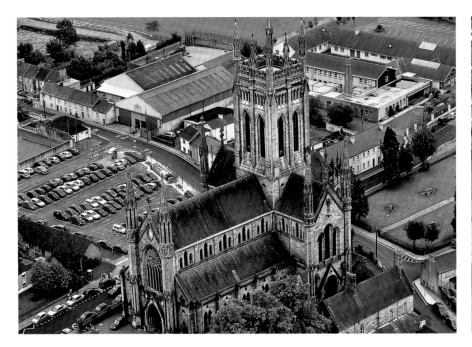

125 The round tower beside St. Canice's Cathedral in the city of Kilkenny was built in the 10th century as part of a monastery that had existed there for hundreds of years. The older parts of the Gothic cathedral date from the 13th century.

126 The city of Waterford was founded as a seaport by Viking settlers in the 10th century on the sheltered waters of the River Suir. It has continued as a major seaport for all of the intervening thousand years. Quaker ship-owners and provision merchants made a great contribution to its welfare.

127 A beautiful modern housing development by the quayside of the River Suir is part of the period of expansion that the ancient city of Waterford – in common with all other cities in Ireland – has experienced since the Celtic Tiger boom of the 1990s.

128 The hilltop Neo-Gothic cathedral, dedicated to the local St Fin-barre in 1879 is one of the most imposing buildings in the city of Cork. Its splendor emphasizes the wealth at the time of the minority Episcopalian Church of Ireland.

129 St Anne Shandon, an early 18th-century church in Cork city is one of the best known in the land, thanks to the poem with the lines 'The bells of Shandon that sound so grand on the pleasant waters of the River Lee.'

IRELAND

SURROUNDED BY WATER

A popular song in the 1960s had the refrain *Thank God we're surrounded by water*. We are and we love it, whether to swim or to sail or to seriously do nothing on a little bit of the countless miles of golden strand. For a relatively small country we have an impressively large coastline – 1970 miles of it. The view from the air is one of tall cliffs standing proud above the boiling surf of the Atlantic, of seemingly endless beaches, of salt marshes and sand flats with their myriads of wild birds and of countless harbors, large and small, with their busy fishing boats and leisure craft of infinite variety.

Within the very bounds of the capital, Dublin Bay offers some of the most varied, spectacular and interesting stretches scenery. And, what is more, it's a scene familiar to most of the inhabitants of the country because passenger planes as they leave or approach Dublin Airport come in low over the bay. It is enclosed to the north by the magnificent headland named Howth by Viking sailors a thousand years ago. At its tip is the Bailey, a rocky promontory, fortified with earthen ramparts by Celtic people, a millennium before the times of the Vikings. And beyond the Bailey, the Kish Lighthouse stands on a sandbank. This imposing tower was built nearby in Dun Laoghaire Harbor and then towed out to its resting place.

North of Howth is the small island called Ireland's Eye, its beach bright with people in summer. Beyond it is the larger and very exclusive Lambay Island, the property of one wealthy man and with a garden designed by Edwin Lutyens. The cliffs are populated by thousands of razorbills, guillemots and kittiwakes, nesting on the rocky ledges. They depart at the end of the summer and stay away at sea until the following spring.

Within the bay the most conspicuous feature is the Great South Wall, running for a mile and a half out into the sea. Begun in 1715, it enjoyed the distinction for many years of being the longest such breakwater in the world. To its north a sandspit, big enough to accommodate two golf links, hugs the shoreline. This, the North Bull Island, is the newest part of the Irish landscape, having grown from a few tiny sandbanks to its present size in less than three hundred years.

Southwards from Dublin, the coast makes a straight line of sand or shingle beach, interrupted now and again by rocky or grassy headlands all the way to the great inlet of Wexford Harbor, close to the southeast corner of Ireland, a place of conflicting sea currents, endlessly at war with each other and sometimes creating and sometimes demolishing sandbanks and islands. North and south of the inlet are walls built in the 19th century to keep out the sea and create huge swathes of grassland. Great flocks of wild geese and ducks assemble there in winter, migrants from the far north.

Between Waterford Harbor and Cork Harbor lies the Copper Coast, so called in honor of centuries of tunneling for metal ores, commemorated by the stone chimneys of abandoned mine workings. The cliff scenery is stupendous. Beyond Cork is Roaringwater Bay, studded with islands large and small, extending to Cape Clear, the most southerly point of Ireland and a haven for naturalists, spotting rare birds, whales and dolphins.

We go around the coast of Kerry, with its long inlets and romantic Blasket and Skellig islands, then north to the Shannon Estuary, the Cliffs of Moher and the Aran Islands and on across Connemara to Clew Bay, said to have an island for every day of the year, and once the fiefdom of the 16th-century pirate-queen Granuaile. North of Clew Bay is Achill Island, the biggest of the islands on the Irish coast and one of the most spectacular, with splendid mountains rising up from the seashore, overlooking a great lake and fantastic strand.

North of Achill is Blacksod Bay and the extraordinary low-lying peninsula of the Mullet, a southerly home for arctic birds. At the north end of the Mullet you turn right to see the incredible cliffs of North Mayo: not as high as the Cliffs of Moher, they go on for much longer, until broken by the Bay of Killala where the forces of the French Republic landed to assist the Irish Revolutionaries in 1798.

The northwestern corner of Ireland is called Bloody Foreland, not an expletive but a reference to the color of its rock. To its east is the Donegal coast, with its distant island of Tory, the home in times long gone of the evil god Balor and, much more recently, of a school of 'primitive' painters. Great inlets penetrate Donegal, the last of them being Lough Swilly, bounded by the mountainous Inishowen Peninsula and Malin Head, the most northerly point of Ireland.

The coast of County Antrim, in Northern Ireland, contrasts with all the others, being much younger geologically and formed of cliffs of white chalk and black basalt, centering on the amazing Giant's Causeway. The east coast of Antrim borders on the Sea of Moyle and is broken by Belfast Lough. South of this inlet are Strangford and Carlingford, both named by the Norsemen of old. The former, almost entirely surrounded by land, is distinguished by the garden of Mount Stewart, one of the most beautiful in Ireland. Carlingford is more open and its seaport, grown up from the Viking trading post, retains its medieval castle walls and delightful pattern of narrow streets. Carlingford Lough lies where the fabled *Mountains of Mourne sweep down to the sea.*

To the south lie miles of sand flats in Dundalk Bay, ending in Clogherhead, one of a great many small harbors with little fishing boats that hunt for the delicious prawns of the Irish Sea. One more promontory, before we return to Howth, is Drumanagh guarded by one of the many squat, circular Martello Towers, built to repel the forces of Napoleon – who never even tried to invade. Our flight around Ireland ends with a particularly impressive view of the long, straight rampart which was built to fortify the headland in ancient Celtic times.

131 Fishing and farming provide a living for people dwelling on the rugged coast of Co. Sligo. Many small harbors were built to accommodate them at the end of the 19th century.

134 Atlantic breakers and floods from the Gweebarra River join forces to create swirling patterns of sea and sand.

135 The Gweebarra, in Co. Donegal, is one of the many west coast rivers which provide food and secure nursery grounds for young migratory trout and salmon which feed and grow in the ocean and later return to spawn. They have provided food for fishing communities for ten thousand years.

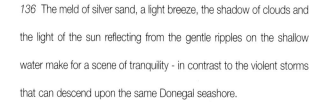

136 The meld of silver sand, a light breeze, the shadow of clouds and the light of the sun reflecting from the gentle ripples on the shallow water make for a scene of tranquility - in contrast to the violent storms that can descend upon the same Donegal seashore.

 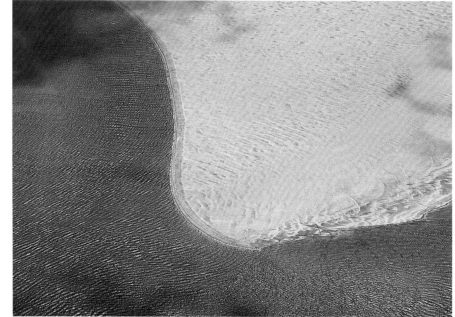

137 Tide, river, sunlight and clumps of green vegetation combine to form a meshwork pattern on a longer finger of sand in the Gwee-barra River.

138 Lighthouses, built of stone, have been functioning on the Irish coast since the 12th century. They serve both to warn mariners of the presence of dangerous rocks and to show a safe passage into harbors and bays.

139 In Co. Donegal a snake-like wall protects the lighthouse compound from unwanted visitors – man and beast. The helicopter pad represents a very much safer and more versatile system for moving in stores and equipment than did the sturdy ships of the past.

140 Rock pinnacles and boiling surf led the 6th-century monk, known as 'Augustine of Ireland' to question the belief that the earth remained unchanged since its creation. He used his scientific observations to show that landscapes evolve over time.

141 Trees and shrubs cannot grow on the low-lying coastal land of Co. Donegal, swept by salt-laden winds. Rocky shores appeal only to visitors who seek solitude - so houses are few and small and tourists rare by this seaside.

142 Between the tongues of rocky shores, in Co. Donegal, small sandy coves abound, so many of them that visitors to Ireland in search of solitude, peace and quiet as well as seaside places have an almost endless choice of havens.

144 Tides and currents, in Co. Donegal, with wind-blown sand produce land forms that change continuously, sometimes growing and forming new islands, sometimes disappearing without a trace and making shapes and patterns of color that rival any artist's work.

145 Tides and winds on the Donegal coast are among the strongest in the world. The receding tide reveals parallel lines of debris deposited by the action of waves. Tidal changes on the Irish coast are dramatic, with a daily range of 13 feet (4 metres) or more.

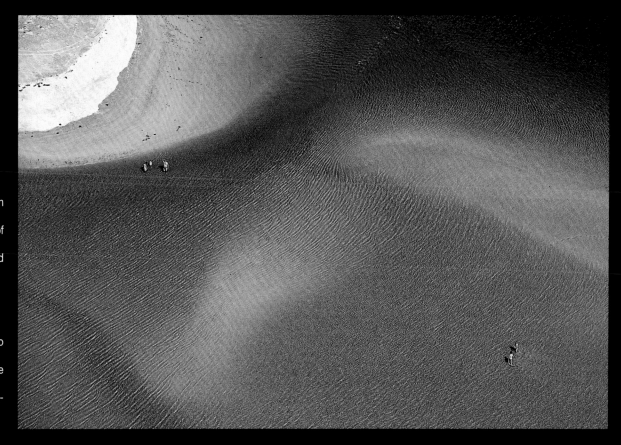

146 Patterns of blue and gold are typical of many seaside place on the Atlantic coast, particularly in Co. Donegal, where great tracts of shoreline have pure, clean sand washed free from the silt deposited by great rivers.

147 The rise and fall of the tides along the Co. Donegal shore, is so great that, where the shore zone is nearly level, the water can recede for a mile (1.6 km) or more. The uninterrupted space and safe, shallow water make such places a haven for young and old alike.

148-149 The rock-girt waters of many coastal regions abound in fish species. Pollack, brilliantly colored wrasse, flounder and many others hunt for marine worms and shellfish, while in summer mackerel enter the shallows as they pursue shoals of smaller species.

150 Joined to the mainland by a causeway, Achill is the biggest island on the Irish coast, distinguished by its magnificent cliffs, lofty mountains and a great strand. It is a very popular summer holiday resort.

151 With magnificent mountain scenery to the south and the long, lonely, low-lying peninsula of the Mullet to the north, Blacksod Bay is renowned as a venue for big-game anglers in search of shark and tuna.

152-153 The coastal lands of Co. Down, on the Irish Sea and overshadowed by the fabled Mountains of Mourne are low-lying and fertile, with large, comfortable farms and many holiday homes.

154 The Atlantic coast of Ireland offers endless variety, particularly in its innumerable inlets and bays. Sligo Bay is a great expanse of shallow water, which strips out at low tide to provide many miles of strand.

155 Horizontal strata of limestone, in Co. Sligo, laid down in a coral sea three hundred million years ago, have weathered to make great level areas of fertile pasture, bordered by a gently sloping rocky foreshore.

156 Sligo is a land of legend and poetry, much of it inspired by its stunningly beautiful landscape both on the coast and inland among lakes and mountains. The foreshore, rocky in places, sandy in others also includes long strips of shingle. Glaciers in the ice age deposited masses of stones and clay. Tidal currents carried the clay away and left the stones behind.

157 Knocknarea, standing sentinel above the coast of Co. Sligo, is topped by Queen Maeve's tomb, a passage grave, constructed five thousand years ago – concealing a burial chamber which has never been opened.

158 Layer upon layer of limestone strata on the Sligo coast testify to millions of years of a steady building up of sediments on the bed of a clear coral sea, in the days when Ireland lay in the tropics, before the movement of continental plates brought it to its present cooler position.

159 Atlantic breakers beat unceasingly at the base of the cliffs of this great promontory of Sligo Bay, slowly but inexorably undermining and carrying away the land. Stone walls separate the properties and divide the fields to allow a rotation of grazing.

160-161 Sandy beaches in sheltered bays on the Atlantic coast mean safe bathing and seaside games for families – and a great many conglomerations of strategically placed mobile homes, sheltered from the westerly wind by the mounting sand dunes.

162 Clew Bay, in Co. Mayo on the west coast of Ireland, is said to have an island for every day of the year. On its southern shore, the beautiful mountain peak of Cruagh Patrick stands out, one of Ireland's holiest shrines and the annual gathering place of thousands of pilgrims.

163 At a time when the sea level was much lower than today, Ice Age glaciers created a range of low hills in the vicinity of Clew Bay. When the ice melted and the sea returned, the hills were transformed to make the mythical 365 islands, large and small.

164 Where the River Moy in Co. Mayo meets the sea at the head of the great Killala Bay, the town of Ballina is growing steadily. Drawn to one of the very best salmon rivers in Ireland, people come from all over Europe and farther afield for the experience of an unequalled fishing holiday.

165 Killala Bay, on the north coast of Co. Mayo, is an inlet 12 miles (20 km) in length. Far from the reach of the authorities in Dublin, it was chosen as a landing place for soldiers from France to support the republican uprising in 1798, known locally ever since as 'The year of the French.'

A VIEW FROM ABOVE

166 The islands and promontories of Clew Bay are composed of clay, sand and gravel rather than solid rock. While the higher parts provide rich pasture, the gravel of the shore line is endlessly carried hither and thither to create fantastic shapes, sculptured by wind and wave.

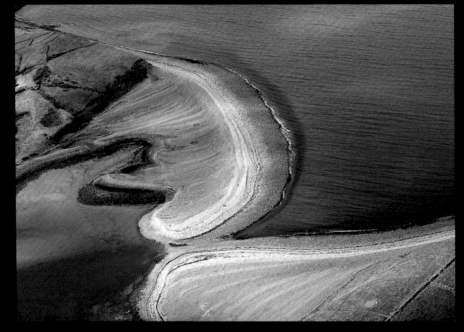

167 Beyond the sculptured shoreline, the seabed in Clew Bay is densely populated by marine worms and shellfish – making it a home for small sharks and giant skate and a paradise for sea anglers.

168 The three Aran Islands lie out in the Atlantic Ocean, forming something of a reef across the entrance to Galway Bay. They are named Inishmore, Inishmaan and Inisheer, from Irish words meaning respectively the big, middle and small islands.

169 Great expanses of level ground are a characteristic of the Aran Islands, resulting from the horizontal strata of the underlying limestone rock. The same structure leads to the development of the splendid cliff scenery on the sides of the islands that face the open ocean.

170 The only village on Inisheer is located in a sheltered bay with a sandy beach. Traditionally, transport from the mainland took place in currachs, canoes of shallow draft with high prows made of cattle hide stretched over timber frames. The 20th-century jetty allows relatively large vessels to land.

171 Much of the land surface of the Aran Islands to this day is covered with stones, with little or no soil. Wonderful wild flowers grow among these stones and include species that are normally found either in Arctic of Mediterranean climates. Both thrive together on Aran.

172 There is a sense of timelessness on the Aran Islands, empha-
sized by the hulk of an oil tanker that ran aground twenty-five years
ago and has remained there ever since. Donkeys rather than cars are
the mainstay of transport on the smaller two islands.

173 The lighthouse on Inisheer used to be tended by two keepers
who lived beside it. Their duties included winding up the weight-driv-
en clockwork mechanism that rotated the lamp, causing it to flash at
regular intervals.

175 The soil in the tiny fields of Inisheer and the other Aran Islands is a mixture of sand and seaweed collected on the shore and carried by the islanders over a period of hundreds of years. The rainfall is low and fresh water accordingly scarce. It is stored in the square tanks within the fields.

176 The west coast of Co. Clare receives the full force of Atlantic Ocean waves. Some of the bays have excellent shelter and beautiful sandy beaches. Over a period of 100 years, people traveled there by the West Clare Railway, immortalized in song by the poet, painter and performer Percy French.

177 Co. Clare has a long seaboard exposed to the Atlantic Ocean. Fishing from the rocks is popular and sharks can be caught - in addition to such very popular species as mackerel and pollack. The rocks can be dangerous because occasionally huge waves roll in from a calm sea.

IRELAND

178 left and center Composed of shales and sandstones, the structure of the Cliffs of Moher leads to the development of magnificent rock pinnacles and stacks. Many thousands of seabirds nest on their ledges in summer.

178 right The Cliffs are justly one of the most popular visitor attractions – as they have been since 1835 when the local landlord built a teahouse in the form of a castle 587 feet (179 m) above the sea.

179 Loop Head is a long rocky promontory which shelters the Shannon Estuary from the force of Atlantic storms. The exposed side has steep cliffs; the land on the sheltered side slopes gently down to the sea. Peat-cutting provided fuel in the past in this treeless region.

180 left and 180-181 The lowlands of the Co. Kerry coast are green and fertile, in contrast to the barren moorlands of the ridges. The shallow waters abound in shellfish and there are great stocks of crab and lobster a little way offshore, making for a major fishing industry.

180 right Parts of Dingle Bay in Co. Kerry have immense sandy beaches, making them popular seaside resorts. The mainland of the Dingle Peninsula is rich with the remains of stone churches and small dwellings.

A VIEW FROM ABOVE

182 left A lonely farm house stands beside a beach, backed by sand dunes in Dingle Bay. The pristine strands attract families to swim and sun-bathe in summer.

182 right In contrast to the sandy beaches, extensive tracts of the shoreline of Dingle Bay offer salt-marsh and creeks. The fishing boat is moored until the right tidal conditions come for its crew to operate their salmon nets.

183 Wildlife abounds in the coastal regions of Co. Kerry. In summer terns, razorbill and guillemot, kittiwake gulls and fulmar petrels come in from the ocean to breed in tens of thousands. Colonies of terns establish themselves on sandy promontories and islands.

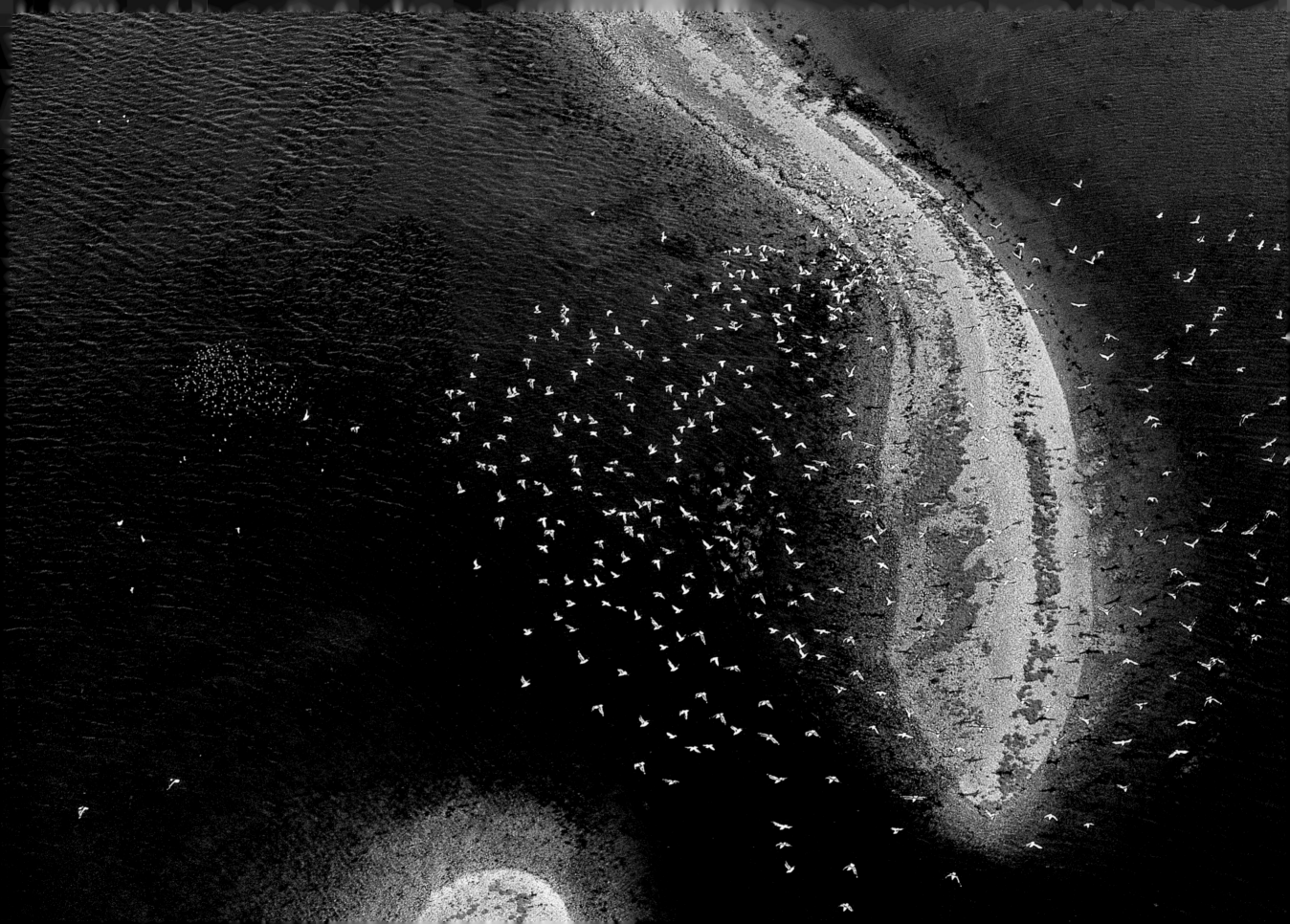

184 The Beara Peninsula is the most southerly of the three great peninsulas of Co. Kerry – and its southern and western regions are in Co. Cork. Castletown Bearhaven was an important British naval base before independence and is now one of the top fishing ports.

185 Copper has been mined on the Beara Peninsula since the Bronze Age, three thousand years ago. The fortunes of a fictional dynasty of mine owners from Cornwall (in England) who managed the mines in recent centuries is the subject of Daphne du Maurier's great novel *Hungry Hills*.

186 The Iveragh Peninsula is bounded to the north by Dingle Bay and to the south by the Kenmare River. Macgillycuddy's Reeks, Ireland's highest mountains, separate it from the rest of Co. Kerry. The Iveragh Peninsula is richly endowed with mountains, lakes and rivers with excellent fishing.

187 The Kerry coastline displays endless variation with much spectacular cliff scenery and many delightful sandy beaches and seaside resorts. Much of the seaboard is within the Gaeltacht, the region of Ireland in which the Irish language, rather than English, is the mother tongue.

IRELAND

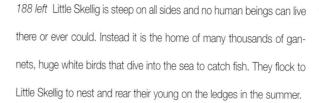

188 left Little Skellig is steep on all sides and no human beings can live there or ever could. Instead it is the home of many thousands of gannets, huge white birds that dive into the sea to catch fish. They flock to Little Skellig to nest and rear their young on the ledges in the summer.

188 right The two Skellig islands stand in the ocean between 5 and 6 miles (7 and 10 km) to the west of Bolus Head on the Iveragh Peninsula. The large one, Skellig Michael, is named in honor of a tradition that the Archangel Michael visited it. Above the old lighthous are the famous ruins of an ancient monastery high on the rock.

189 The lighthouse on Skellig Michael stands high above the sea, surrounded by the nests of many seabirds. These birds, kittiwake gulls and several others, spend the greater part of every year far from the land, returning only in summer to rear their families.

190 Fastnet Rock supports one of the most isolated and most beautiful of Irish lighthouses. It stands on a tiny speck of rock, 8 miles (13 km) to the southwest of Brow Head, the most southerly point of Ireland. The annual Fastnet race for sailing boats is one of the most celebrated in Europe.

191 Steep sea cliffs are the ultimate wilderness in Ireland, the only part of the landscape whose appearance has not been altered by the hand of men. Even islands and mountain-tops are grazed by sheep – but neither humans nor their plants and animals can survive on the bare rock.

192 Mizen Head on the coast of Co. Cork is only a few hundred yards short of being the most southerly point of the mainland of Ireland. Its close, but much less spectacular, neighbor Brow Head claims that honor at Latitude 51°26' North.

193 Intense folding in the Old Red Sandstone strata of south Cork has produced the marvelous rock ridges and caves that characterise Mizen Head. This same folding on the grand scale formed the parallel mountain ranges of Cork and Kerry and their great sea inlets to the west.

195 The Metal Man of Tramore, on the Waterford coast, stands on the central tower of the three built on Great Newtown Head in 1819 to the design of the Scottish engineer Alexander Nimmo. They are one of a series of beacons which identify important headlands for mariners.

IRELAND
FRIENDLY TOWNS AND VILLAGES

For seventy years, the center of the known universe was located in the garden of a great house in a small town in the midlands of Ireland. Like other small towns, Birr has a carefully planned layout, with tree-lined roadsides, elegant homes and, close by, a large house in the form of a mock castle with a huge garden and an ornamental lake. Birr Castle is different in that it has a colossal telescope as a larger-than-life garden ornament. Its owner, the Third Earl of Rosse, was a man of genius with a particular interest in astronomy. The telescopes of his day were not big enough for him – so he built his own, with the help of the workmen on his estate, in 1842. It was the largest in the world and held its place for the next seventy years. Abandoned for a while, it was recently brought back to life.

Other villages, while they don't have telescopes, have real castles and the very best known of them is Blarney, not far from the city of Cork. Fly low over it and you will enjoy the extraordinary sight of a rooftop crowded with people queuing up to lean backwards over the parapet and kiss the Blarney Stone which, from time immemorial, has been most inconveniently located there. Those who kiss it will be granted unimagined powers of 'blarneying,' the ability to talk oneself out of any difficult situation. The castle and the woods that surround it are a beautiful sight, as is the busy village that grew up in their shade.

Birr is a well-ordered town, the result of planning by the landlord in the 18th century. Blarney is a village that grew in its own sweet way, without any interference from a noble town planner. They represent two trends in Irish life, the one well-disciplined, the other rejoicing in its freedom. But the Irish character, though always charming, is never simple and the best of the planned towns always have areas of spontaneity and the most haphazard of villages display some kind of form – there is endless room for compromise.

The extreme of the unplanned entity is known to very few people. While the majority of villages in Ireland have grown up on either side of a road which is heading somewhere, Licketstown lies at the end of a road – which is why nobody ever goes through it on their way to anywhere else. Not far from the bustling city of Waterford, the village is close to the banks of the River Suir and consists of a totally charming collection of thatched cottages.

Thatched roofs, made from straw or from tall reed stems, were the rule in rural Ireland. Thatch is pretty and warm and dampens the sound of the rain when it falls – but it doesn't last forever and the cost of renewing it led to a take-over by tiles. As well as in Licketstown, thatch prevails in Adare, without doubt the prettiest village in Ireland. It was conceived by Lord Dunraven in the 19th century – but he adopted the old-time straggling village that had grown up on his property and had the houses rebuilt and improved, while still following the old layout and still retaining their thatched roofs. There were no fewer than three ruined monasteries in the village and he had parts of two of these rebuilt to serve as Protestant and Catholic churches. Visitors flock there today and the picturesque cottages have adapted themselves to the needs of book sellers and antique dealers. The name of the village is Adare and it complies with tradition by having a magnificent manorial dwelling and beautiful parkland and gardens by its side.

Villages and towns, as we know them, came to be established in Ireland over the course of the 12th century by the descendants of the Anglo-Norman settlers rather than by the Celtic people. Two of their greatest foundations are Trim, in the midlands, and Carrickfergus on the northeast coast. These towns began with castles which, after more than 800 years, still dominate the scene. While the Celtic chieftains lived in scattered, fortified homesteads their contemporaries in the monasteries did develop large, settled communities, in some cases inhabited by thousands of monks, nuns and students. In effect they served as universities. Many of them are known only by name, but some present a wonderful scene from the air, commemorating more than a thousand years of sanctity and peace. One of the greatest is Clonmacnoise, founded in 540. T W Rolleston described it in these lines: *In a quiet, water'd land, a land of roses, lies St. Kieran's city fair; and the warriors of Erin in their famous generations slumber there.* Clonmacnoise lies amongst green fields in a bend on the River Shannon and retains a round tower and two Celtic crosses as well as the ruins of a cathedral and a great collection of sculptures from the Dark Ages.

A more recent ecclesiastical establishment is Maynooth, a town in the midlands which grew up in the shadow of its Anglo-Norman castle but was embellished in the 18th century by the Earl of Kildare who built himself a splendid house nearby and joined his demesne to the town by a beautiful avenue of linden trees. In 1795 a Catholic seminary was built, centered on Classical and Neo-Gothic buildings, dominated by the splendid tower and spire that stand beside the church. Still the center of Catholic teaching in Ireland, the seminary in 1966 opened its doors as a university college for women as well as men.

Medieval monks, then settlers and invaders and, later still, peaceful landlords made the most of the towns and villages of Ireland. Here and there smaller groups established their own communities. Amongst them were the Quakers who built factories and at the same time made houses for their workers, together with a school for everybody and a meeting house for themselves. Ballitore is one such, where the view from above is of the modest meeting house and the foundations of the school which, during a period of religious intolerance, educated together the rebel leader Napper Tandy, the immortal Parliamentarian Edmund Burke and the Archbishop Cardinal Cullen.

197 Ballyshannon developed rapidly in the 19th century and one or more Gothic-revival churches stand surrounded by neat two- and three-story town houses. The majority of 20th-century homes and shops lie on the periphery of the older town center.

200 The promontory of Ramore is a nature reserve and makes a pleasing contrast with the busy resort buildings of Portrush. Ramore is one of a number of spectacular headlands on the Antrim coast, most famous of all being the nearby World Heritage Center at the Giant's Causeway.

201 Around the sea-front at Portrush are numerous hotels, together with one of he greatest amusement parks in Ireland and an indoor water-world with water flumes, water cannon, jacuzzis and many other forms of entertainment.

202-203 Situated on the narrow promontory of Ramore on the north coast of Co. Antrim, Portrush is a very popular seaside resort which developed when the railway reached it in the 19th century. The older houses were built at the same time as the railway to cater for the increasing numbers of visitors.

204 left Killybegs is the principal fishing port on the northwest coast of Ireland, on the edge of the Atlantic ocean, but sheltered from its gales by surrounding hills and the small island with its lighthouse.

204 right and 205 The busy harbor of Killybegs caters for all kinds of fishing vessels, from small locally-built boats with wooden hulls to giant super-trawlers that travel to distant fishing grounds, processing their catch on board. Food-processing factories provide a back-up for the fishing industry.

206 In the center of Enniskillen in Co. Fermanagh stands the Anglican cathedral; facing it across the street from a hilltop overlooking the River Erne is the Catholic cathedral. Below them by the riverside is the military barracks, with fortifications going back to the 16th century.

207 A delightful variety of 19th-century houses and shops are crowded together on the steep hillsides of the town of Enniskillen. For centuries the town was a strategic point, guarding a crossing place on the River Erne.

208 Co. Donegal is named after Donegal town whose Irish name translates as the 'Fort of the Foreigners' and refers to the Viking settlers who established it as a seaport in medieval times.

209 Beside the church of Ballyshannon is the grave of the 19th century poet William Allingham who celebrated the town and its beautiful surroundings in very popular poetry. Set on the steep banks of the River Erne it commanded the borders of Co. Donegal.

210 On a hilltop overlooking a bend in the River Erne, the cathedral dedicated to the local St Macartan dates to the 17th century. It was built with plenty of space surrounding it to serve as a burial ground.

211 One of the most beautifully situated towns in Ireland, Enniskillen grew up from medieval fortifications on an island between Upper and Lower Lough Erne. Over the centuries it has grown to occupy many islands and promontories.

212 On the edge of the village of Hillsborough in Co. Down is the splendid classical house and extensive parkland created by the descendants
of Sir Moyses Hill in the 18th century. It has been the venue for vital con-
ferences between the British and Irish governments over the future of
Northern Ireland.

214-215 The Mullet Peninsula is a great area of low-lying land on the
west coast of Co. Mayo. The village developed rapidly from a hamlet
of three houses to a thriving community early in the 19th century, when
a canal was cut across the narrow neck of the isthmus.

213 Located on the edge of mountainous country in Co. Down, Hillsborough is named not because of the terrain, but to commemorate the
family name of its 17th century founder Sir Moyses Hill. The 18th-centu-
ry Gothic-revival church is one of many splendid buildings in the village.

216 The round tower in the center of Killala was built in the 10th century and is the last remnant of a monastery which flourished at that time. It is a busy fishing port, the base for boats which harvest the rich stocks of fish in Killala Bay and which cater for visiting game fishermen.

217 The town of Ballina crosses the River Moy where it begins to widen towards the sea and the great Killala Bay. The largest town in Co. Mayo, it is something of a gateway to the great wilderness of Bangor Erris and much of the finest and least known cliff scenery in Ireland.

218 A new marina and new holiday homes, beside the River Shannon in the old town of Carrick-on-Shannon, testify to an explosion in popularity of boating, fishing and other river-based recreation in the course of the second half of the 20th century.

219 Carrick-on Shannon, the capital of Co. Leitrim, is a major centre for pleasure boating and fishing in the waters and nearby small lakes of the Shannon. These form part of the magnificent Shannon-Erne waterway which extends for 185 miles (300 km).

220 One of the biggest and most important towns of the midlands, Mullingar in Co. Westmeath developed as the marketing center of the cattle industry in the region. It lies in a region of beautiful lakes, green hills and woodland.

221 The large and imposing Cathedral of Christ the King, surrounded by church-run colleges, is the dominant building of Mullingar. It was built in 1936 and its museum contains vestments which belonged to the 17th century martyr St Oliver Plunket.

222-223 The village of Clifden, on the barren west coast of Galway, was established in 1812 by John D'Arcy, a landlord from the fertile east of the county. He believed that there was scope for development on the western seaboard and accordingly founded a settlement and encourage people to go there.

224 Far out on the peninsula of the same name, the town of Dingle is one of the most important centers within the Gaeltacht, the region of Ireland in which the Gaelic language is in regular use. Its official name is its Irish form An Daingean or Daingean Uí Chúis.

225 The ancient harbor of Dingle was extended and modernized in the 1960s and is now one of the premier fishing ports of Ireland. The fleet operates over a huge expanse of ocean to the south-west which includes some of the richest fishing grounds on the Atlantic seaboard.

226 Killarney became established as a tourist centre in the 19th century and remains the best-known of all of Ireland's resorts, famous in song and story and the setting for plays and operas. St Mary's Cathedral, begun in 1842, is one of Pugin's finest Irish designs.

227 The lakes and mountains of the Killarney Valley in Co. Kerry are among the most beautiful in Ireland. The country is of particular interest in preserving oak woodland and wild red deer descended from the original native stock, extinct elsewhere in the country.

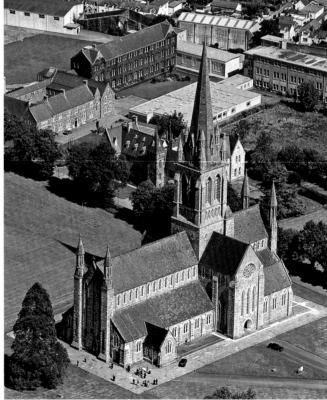

228-229 On the high ground overlooking the valley of the River Blackwater in Co. Waterford, the village of Lismore lies in the shadow of the great 19th century castellated mansion. The great scientist Robert Boyle, the 'father of chemistry' was born there in 1627.

230 The quayside of Cobh on Great Island in the huge sea inlet called Cork Harbor lies at the foot of a steep hill. Streets and houses built in the 19th century are arranged in tiers in the absence of extensive level ground.

231 Begun in 1868 to the design of Edward Welby Pugin and George C. Ashlin, the magnificent hillside cathedral of Cobh was not completed until 1949. It has a carillon of 42 bells, the largest in Ireland.

233 St Colman's Cathedral in Cobh looks out over the harbor which developed in the 18th century, first as a naval base at the time of warfare with America and France. It became a place of tragic partings for more than a century, as people fled from the famine-stricken west.

234 The town of Bantry stands at the head of Bantry Bay, one of the great inlets on the coast of Co. Cork. For centuries an important naval base – it was twice attacked by French fleets and once the scene of a mutiny on a British man-o' war – it is now a peaceful centre for shellfish-farming.

235 Bantry to-day is a popular tourist resort and a center for exploring the beautiful west-Cork scenery that surrounds it. The nearby Bantry House is a magnificent 18th-century mansion and an important concert venue.

236 Now a small and delightful holiday resort, Baltimore enjoyed a long period of fame as a strategic coastal defense in time past. It was occupied by Spanish invaders in 1602 and in 1631 pirates seized 200 of is inhabitants and carried them off to Algeria.

237 Baltimore is a fishing village and yachting harbor with a long-established shipyard and a reputation for building fine sailing craft. It caters for the neighboring islands of Sherkin and Cape Clear. These are the biggest islands of the nearby Roaringwater Bay, a shallow inlet with many islands.

INDEX

PHOTO CREDITS

All photographs are by Antonio Attini/Archivio White Star, except the following:

Page 1 Livio Bourbon/Archivio White Star
Page 99 www.jasonhawkes.com
Pages 102 and 102-103 www.jasonhawkes.com
Page 113 Atlantide S.N.C./Agefotostock/Marka
Page 121 www.jasonhawkes.com
Page 226 bottom left www.jasonhawkes.com
Page 227 www.jasonhawkes.com

240 Separating eastern pasture from western wilderness, Lough Corrib is

an angler's paradise, teeming with splendid trout and pike.